AGE 5-7

Spelling
Skills

Exercises devised by Brenda Aps
an experienced author and editor who spec
in writing early learning books for childre
Illustrated by John Haslam

Learning Rewards is a home-learning programme designed to help your child succeed at school with the National Curriculum. It has been extensively researched with parents and teachers.

This book, *Spelling Skills*, and its companion title, *Spelling Practice*, cover important aspects of the National Curriculum at Key Stage I.

Children should start with the *Skills* books (with younger children this is important) and progress to the *Practice* books.

The *Skills* book teaches basic skills and new concepts through structured and enjoyable activities. The *Practice* book reinforces and builds on these skills by the essential repetition of exercises.

You will need to work through each page with your child and talk about what is required. The content is progressive, so start from the front of the book.

The fold-out progress chart is a useful record of your child's performance. Always reward your child's work with encouragement and a gold star sticker.

When you come to the end of the book you will find a fun, wipe-clean learning game.

Key to symbols on the page:

skills covered by each exercise as they relate to the National Curriculum

notes for parents, explaining specific teaching points

follow-up activities which will extend your child's understanding of the exercise

series editor: Nina Filipek
series designer: Paul Dronsfield
designer: Hilary Edwards-Malam
Copyright © 1996 World International Limited.
All rights reserved.
Published in Great Britain by
World International Limited, Deanway Technology Centre,
Wilmslow Road, Handforth, Cheshire SK9 3FB.
Printed in Italy.
ISBN 0 7498 2705 X

First-letter sounds

To recognise first-letter sounds and spell simple words.

Write the first letters to spell the words.
The pictures will help you.
There is one word for each letter of the alphabet.
Cross out the alphabet letters as you write them.

a b c d e f g h i j k l

ant

bee

cat

dog

egg

fish

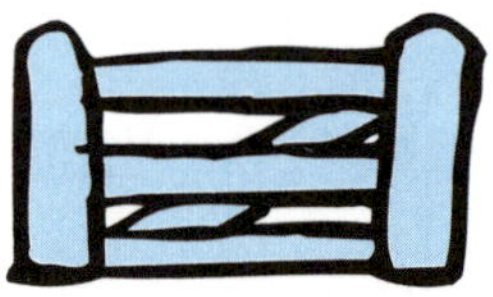

gate

hat

ink

jug

kite

log

When sounding out the first letters say the phonic sounds, not the letter names.

To recognise first-letter sounds and spell simple words.

First-letter sounds

m n o p q r s t u v w x y z

_op

_et

_range

_an

_ueen

_ug

_un

_oy

_p

_an

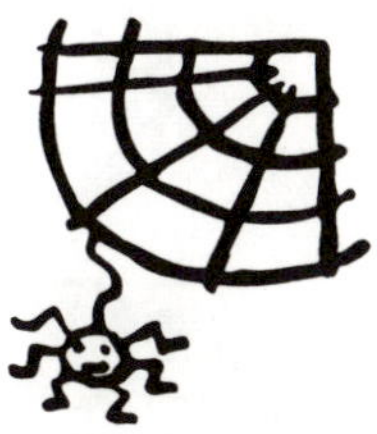
_eb

_-ray

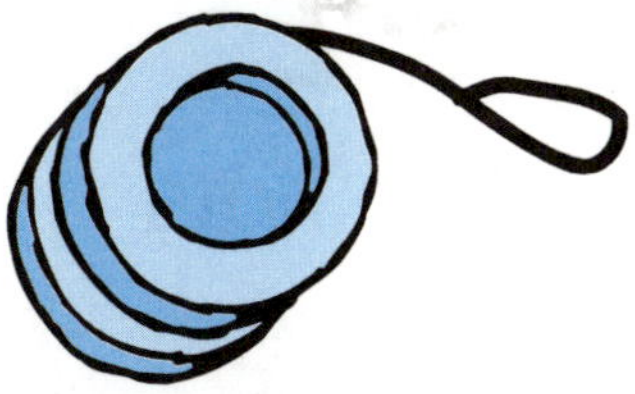
_o-yo

_ip

Words with a

To spell words with the **a** sound.

Write **a** to spell the words. Spell each word twice.

v _ n

c _ p

j _ m

b _ g

m _ n

h _ t

c _ t

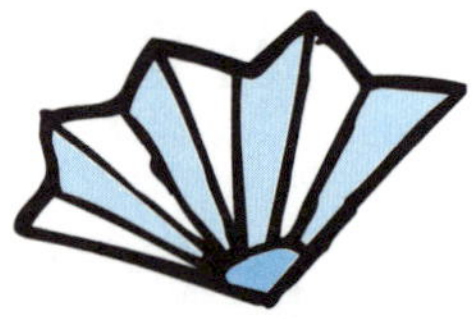

f _ n

Choose the right words. Spell them.

The cat sat on the _ _ _ .

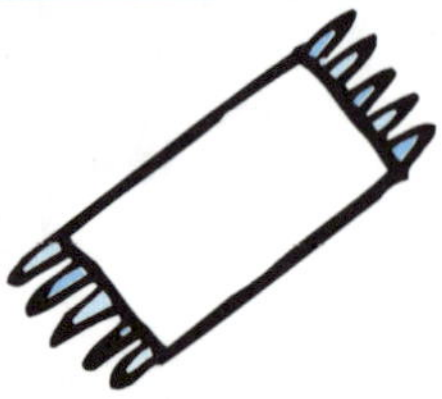

fat hat mat

The man has a _ _ _ .

pan hat map

The _ _ _ is black.

sat hat bat

Here are six _ _ _ _ .

cats hats mats

The vowel **a** has a short, hard sound in these words.

To spell words with the **e** sound.

Words with e

Write **e** to spell the words. Spell each word twice.

b _ d
_ _ _

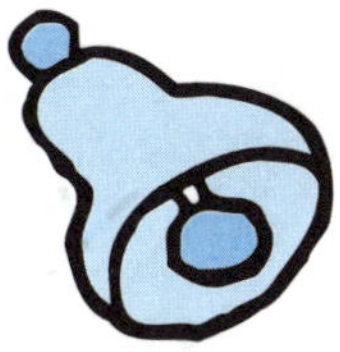
b _ l l
_ _ _ _

p _ g
_ _ _

t _ n
_ _ _

n _ t
_ _ _

h _ n
_ _ _

n _ s t
_ _ _ _

t _ d d y
_ _ _ _ _

Choose the right words. Spell them.

The table has four _ _ _ _ .  legs pegs beds

Here are three _ _ _ _ .  hens eggs pens

The teddy is on the _ _ _ .  net red bed

Here are _ _ _ pegs.  ten beds pegs

The vowel **e** has a short, hard sound in these words.

Words with i, o and u

To spell words with **i**, **o** and **u** sounds.

Write **i** to spell the words. Spell each word twice.

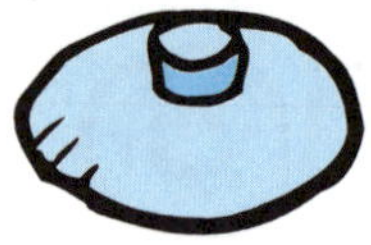

l _ d

_ _ _

p _ n

_ _ _

z _ p

_ _ _

b _ n

_ _ _

w _ g

_ _ _

b _ b

_ _ _

h _ l l

_ _ _ _

k _ n g

_ _ _ _

Write **o** to spell the words. Spell each word twice.

c _ t

_ _ _

d _ g

_ _ _

m _ p

_ _ _

p _ t

_ _ _

h _ p

_ _ _

d _ l l

_ _ _ _

b _ x

_ _ _

t _ p

_ _ _

The vowels **i**, **o** and **u** have a short, hard sound in these words.

To spell words with **i**, **o** and **u** sounds.

Words with i, o and u

Write **u** to spell the words. Spell each word twice.

c _ p
_ _ _

t _ b
_ _ _

b _ n
_ _ _

s _ n
_ _ _

m _ m
_ _ _

s _ m
_ _ _

h _ t
_ _ _

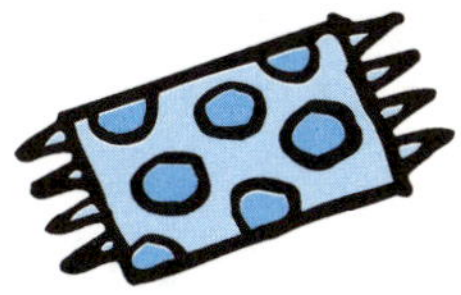
r _ g
_ _ _

Choose the right words. Spell them.

The _ _ _ is in the sky.

bun top sun

The bag has a _ _ _ .
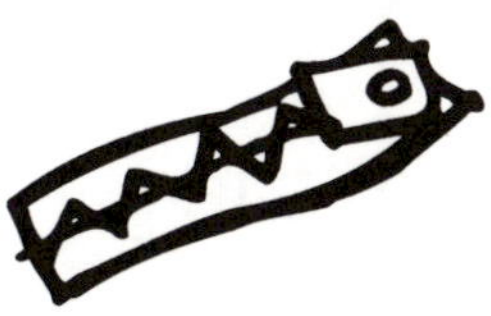
zip cup pup

Here is a _ _ _ .

tip cup lip

The dog is _ _ _ .

pip bib big

Simple, single syllable words are the first words your child will be able to read and spell.

Words with ck and st

To spell words with the letters **ck** and **st**.

Do the letter sums to spell the **ck** words.
Draw lines to match the words to the pictures.

du + ck = ____

so + ck = ____

ki + ck = ____

sa + ck = ____

ne + ck = ____

The letters **st** can start and end words.
Write the words that finish the sentences.
Choose from the list.

last start first stop fast step lost

Dan ran fast right from the ______ .

He came ______ in the race.

Ben ran slowly. He came _____ .

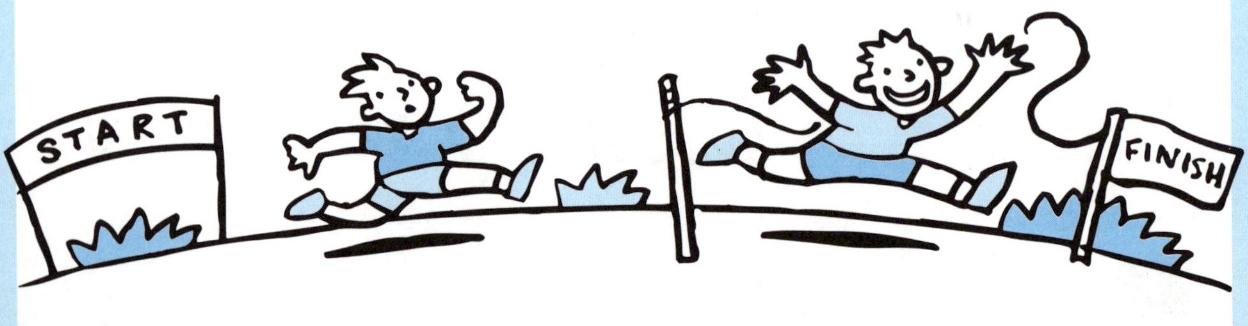

☆ To spell words with the letters **ch**, **sh** and **th**.

Words with ch, sh, th

Write **ch** or **sh** to spell the words. Spell each word twice.

fi_ _

_ _ _ _

_ _imp

_ _ _ _ _

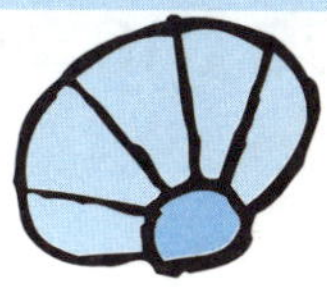

_ _ell

_ _ _ _ _

_ _air

_ _ _ _ _

_ _ip

_ _ _ _

_ _ur_ _

_ _ _ _ _ _

Choose the right **th** words. Spell them.

My parents are my _ _ _ _ _ _ _ and _ _ _ _ _ _ _ .

mother brother father

I like having a _ _ _ _ .

mother bath path

The shark has sharp _ _ _ _ _ .

teeth them think

The _ _ _ _ was very steep.

there the path

Words with 'magic e'

To recognise how words change when **e** is added.

When the letter **e** is added to the end of a word it changes the word. So **man** becomes **mane**.

+ e =

Add '**magic e**' to make new words.

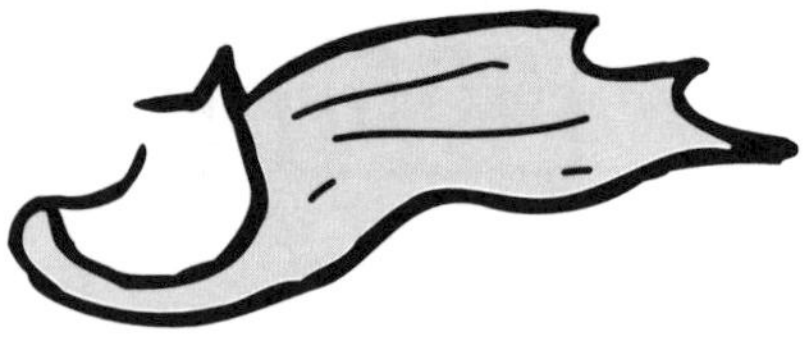

cap + e = _ _ _ _

tap + e = _ _ _ _

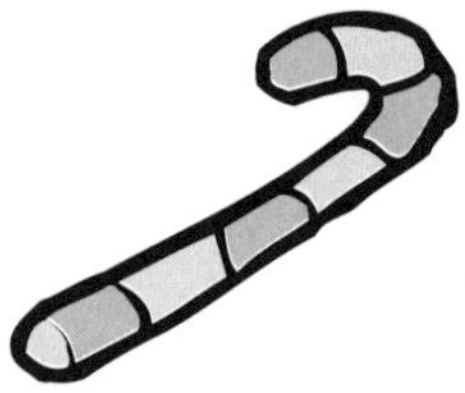

can + e = _ _ _ _

pan + e = _ _ _ _

Add '**magic e**' to make new words.
Draw lines to match the old word with the new word.

pin _

tub _

cub _

tube 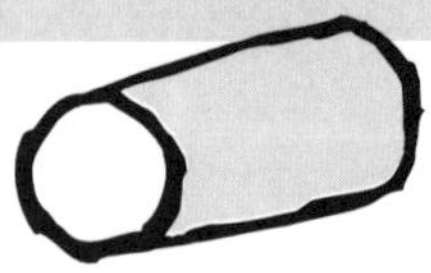

cube 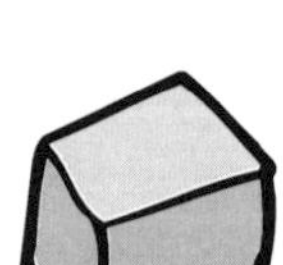

pine 

The '**magic e**' changes the sound of the vowel from a short sound to a long sound.

To recognise how words change when **e** is added.

Words with 'magic e'

Find these '**magic e**' words in the wordsquare.
Look left to right, right to left, up and down.
The first word is done to show you how.

bone

mole

hole

home

nose

pole

robe

rose

stone

a	h	o	l	e	d	f
m	a	e	n	o	t	s
r	p	o	l	e	z	g
o	e	i	r	o	b	e
s	q	h	j	x	o	s
e	m	o	h	y	n	o
k	s	m	o	l	e	n

Older children might be able to think of more examples of '**magic e**' words. They could list them in a spelling book.

Words with bl, cl, fl, gl, pl, sl

To spell words that begin with **bl**, **cl**, **fl**, **gl**, **pl** and **sl**.

Match the letters to spell words. Spell each word twice.

bl

_ _ a c k   _ _ o c k   _ _ i n k

_ _ _ _ _   _ _ _ _ _   _ _ _ _ _

cl

_ _ a p   _ _ a y   _ _ i p

_ _ _ _   _ _ _ _   _ _ _ _

fl

_ _ a g   _ _ y   _ _ a t

_ _ _ _   _ _ _   _ _ _ _

gl

_ _ a s s   _ _ u e   _ _ o v e

_ _ _ _ _   _ _ _ _   _ _ _ _ _

pl

_ _ a y   _ _ u m   _ _ a n t

_ _ _ _   _ _ _ _   _ _ _ _ _

sl

_ _ o w   _ _ i p   _ _ e e _

_ _ _ _   _ _ _ _   _ _ _ _ _

Read the first two letters together as **one** sound.

To spell words that begin with **br**, **cr**, **dr**, **fr**, **gr** and **tr**.

Words with br, cr, dr, fr, gr, tr

Match the letters to spell words. Spell each word twice.

br

_ _ ick
_ _ _ _ _

_ _ idge
_ _ _ _ _ _

_ _ im
_ _ _ _

cr

_ _ ab
_ _ _ _

_ _ y
_ _ _

_ _ eam
_ _ _ _ _

dr

_ _ ip
_ _ _ _

_ _ ess
_ _ _ _ _

_ _ aw
_ _ _ _

fr

_ _ og
_ _ _ _

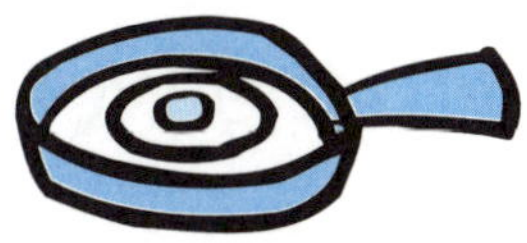
_ _ y
_ _ _

_ _ ost
_ _ _ _ _

gr

_ _ ow
_ _ _ _

_ _ ape
_ _ _ _ _

_ _ ass
_ _ _ _ _

tr

_ _ ee
_ _ _ _

_ _ ain
_ _ _ _ _

_ _ ick
_ _ _ _ _

Can you think of any more words that begin with these sounds?

Words with double letters

To spell words with double letters.

Write **oo** to spell the words.
Draw lines to match the words to the pictures.

s p _ _ n

m _ _ n

b _ _ t

b a l l _ _ n

s c h _ _ l

Write **ee** to finish the spelling sums.
Draw lines to match the words and pictures.

b + e e = _ _ _

f + e e + t = _ _ _ _

t r + e e = _ _ _ _

p + e e + p = _ _ _ _

s l + e e + p = _ _ _ _ _

To spell words with double letters.

Words with double letters

Spell the double letter words.
Choose the letters from the list.

ff
ll
pp
rr
ss
tt

to _ _ ee	fi _ _	pe _ _ er
na _ _ y	ba _ _	be _ _
pa _ _ ot	pu _ _ y	ki _ _ en
gra _ _	gla _ _	hi _ _
lo _ _ y	ca _ _ ot	wa _ _

Read the rhyme. Underline all the double letter words.
Look for **ee**, **ll**, **mm** and **tt**.

Three little kittens they lost their mittens,
And they began to cry.
"Oh, Mummy dear, we greatly fear,
Our mittens we have lost."
"What? Lost your mittens?
You naughty kittens! Now you shall have no pie!"

Words with qu

To spell words that begin with **qu**.

The letter **u** always comes after the letter **q**.
The letters **qu** sound like *kw* as in queen.
Read this story. Underline all the **qu** words you can find.

"Quick!" said the queen. "It's a quarter-past seven. Turn on the TV. There's a new quiz show I want to watch. Quickly now!"

The king turned on the TV, but he didn't watch the quiz show. He lay on the sofa under a warm quilt. It was quite warm, and soon the king was fast asleep. He started to snore.

"Be quiet!" the queen cried. "I can't hear the questions!"

"Shan't!" said the king.

Oh dear, do you think they were going to have a quarrel?

To spell words that begin with **kn** and **wh**.

Silent letters kn and wh

The letters **kn** make the sound of *n*. The **k** is always 'silent'. You write it but you do not say it.
Write **kn** to spell the words.
Draw lines to match the words to the pictures.

_ _ee

_ _ife

_ _ot

_ _it

_ _ob

The letters **wh** sound like *w*. The letter **h** is 'silent'.
Write **wh** to spell the words.
Lots of **wh** words ask questions.
Draw circles around the words that ask questions.

_ _eel   _ _y   _ _at   _ _ite

_ _en   _ _ere   _ _ich   _ _isper

Do you know of any other words with silent letters, e.g. comb, wrap, ghost?

Words with oa and ow

To spell words with **oa** and **ow**.

The letters **oa** and **ow** both sound like *o* in these words. Choose the right words from the lists. Spell them.

foal
goat
moat
loaf
soap
boat

A _ _ _ _ of bread.

A _ _ _ _ is a baby horse.

A _ _ _ _ goes on water.

I wash with _ _ _ _ .

slow
grows
mows
crow
blow
snows

A _ _ _ _ snail.

A black _ _ _ _ .

I _ _ _ _ out my candles.

It _ _ _ _ _ in winter.

To spell words with **ou** and **ow**.

Words with ou and ow

The letters **ou** and **ow** sound the same in these words.
Choose the right words from the lists. Spell them.

- loud
- house
- pound
- out
- shout
- mound

In and _ _ _ .

100 pence make 1 _ _ _ _ _ .

I live in a _ _ _ _ _ .

The music is _ _ _ _ .

- cow
- down
- owl
- frown
- towel
- clown

An _ _ _ is a bird with big eyes.

A _ _ _ gives us milk.

Up and _ _ _ _ .

I dry myself with a _ _ _ _ _ .

There is no spelling rule to follow here.
Children should learn these words by heart.

Words with ai

☆ To spell words with **ai**.

Write **ai** to spell these words. Spell each word twice.

t _ _ l
_ _ _ _

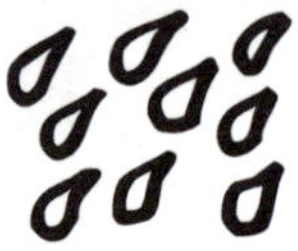
r _ _ n
_ _ _ _

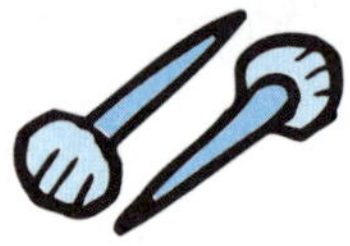
n _ _ l
_ _ _ _

gr _ _ n
_ _ _ _ _

tr _ _ n
_ _ _ _ _

sn _ _ l
_ _ _ _ _

h _ _ r
_ _ _ _

ch _ _ r
_ _ _ _ _

Choose the right words. Spell them.

Brush your _ _ _ _ .

hair fair chair

Jack and Jill went to get a _ _ _ _ of water.

rail pail bail

We went to the _ _ _ _ .

fair mail gain

The postman delivers _ _ _ _ .

snail mail grain

To spell words with **ea**.

Words with ea

Some words with **ea** have a l-o-n-g sound, as in **east**. Some words with **ea** have a short sound, as in **head**. Look at the words and pictures. Which **ea** sound do they have? Spell the words on the lines.

teacher

seat

teapot

feather

treasure

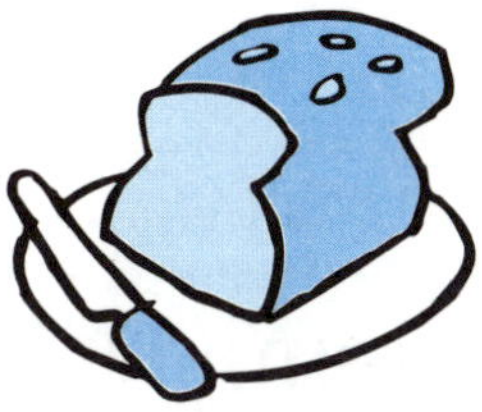

bread

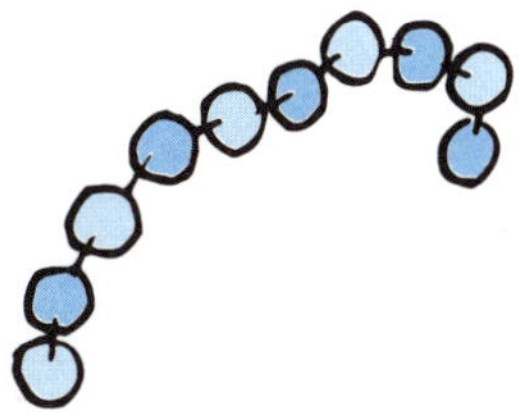

beads

head

l-o-n-g **ea** as in east

short **ea** as in head

Read out each word clearly. Listen for the sound of **ea**.
Is it a long sound or a short sound?

Words that end with ay

To spell words that end with **ay**.

Write **ay** to spell the words. Spell each word twice.

h _ _
_ _ _

b _ _
_ _ _

t r _ _
_ _ _ _

p l _ _
_ _ _ _

c l _ _
_ _ _ _

r _ _
_ _ _

p _ _
_ _ _

p r _ _
_ _ _ _

Choose the right words. Spell them.

Boys and girls go out to _ _ _ _ .

pay   play   say

We make models with _ _ _ _ .

clay   hay   bay

Can you _ _ _ the letters of the alphabet?

say   may   lay

The hen _ _ _ _ eggs.

says   lays   prays

To spell words that end with **ight**.

Words that end with ight

The letters **ight** make a sound like *ite*. The **g** and **h** are 'silent' letters. Write **ight** to spell the words. Spell each word twice.

n _ _ _ _

_ _ _ _ _ _

r _ _ _ _

_ _ _ _ _ _

f _ _ _ _

_ _ _ _ _ _

l _ _ _ _

_ _ _ _ _ _

k n _ _ _ _

_ _ _ _ _ _ _

f r _ _ _ _

_ _ _ _ _ _ _

Choose the right words. Spell them.

The stars are _ _ _ _ _ _ _ .

bright might

Left and _ _ _ _ _ _ .

fight right

The plane set off on its _ _ _ _ _ _ _ .

flight fight

How tall you are is your _ _ _ _ _ _ _ .

sight height

Adding ing

To spell verbs when **ing** is added.

Lots of verbs or doing words end in **ing**.
For example, **walking** and **jumping** are verbs.
When you add **ing** to a verb that ends in **e**, the **e** disappears. For example: **I make** but **I am making**.

m a k e + i n g = m a k i n g

Spell these words by adding **ing**.

We skate. We are _ _ _ _ _ _ _ _ .

She bakes. She is _ _ _ _ _ _ _ .

They wave. They are _ _ _ _ _ _ _ .

I dance. I am _ _ _ _ _ _ _ _ .

He drives. He is _ _ _ _ _ _ _ _ .

Choose the right **ing** words from the list. Spell them.

hoping sliding biting using writing taking

I am _ _ _ _ _ a pencil and ruler to draw a line.

I am _ _ _ _ _ _ to get a computer for my birthday.

In winter I like _ _ _ _ _ _ _ on the ice.

To spell verbs when **ing** is added.

Adding ing

Look what happens to these words when we add **ing**.

hop + ing = hopping

shop + ing = shopping

run + ing = running

clap + ing = clapping

swim + ing = swimming

Choose the right **ing** words from the list.
Spell them.

sipping cutting getting winning letting hitting

I am _ _ _ _ _ _ _ _ ready for bed.

I am _ _ _ _ _ _ _ _ my drink.

I am _ _ _ _ _ _ _ _ some paper.

With older children, point to the vowel before the last letter to explain the spelling rule.

Adding s

To spell plurals with **s** and **es** endings.

A plural word is one that means more than one of something, as in **boys**.
Some words are made into plural words by adding **s** at the end.
Spell the plural words by adding **s**.

one ball  two ______ 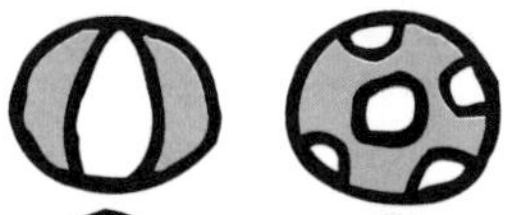

one bun  two ____ 

one mug  two ____ 

Some words are made into plural words by adding **es** at the end. This happens when the words end in **ch**, **sh**, **s**, **ss** or **x**.
Spell the plural words by adding **es**.

one brush  two ________ 

one dress  two ________ 

one dish  two _______ 

Spell the plural word for each set of things.

 ______

 ____

 ________

To spell plurals ending **ies** and plurals that do not follow rules.

Adding s

To spell plurals of some words that end in the letter **y**, add **s**. For example, one **day** and two **days**.
For some words that end in **y** write **ies** instead of **y**: one **party**, two **parties**.
Spell the plural words by writing **ies** instead of **y**.

one fly  two fl _ _ _ 

one lady  two _ _ _ _ _ _ _ 

one fairy  two _ _ _ _ _ _ _ _ 

The plural words for some things are quite different.
Read the words. Draw lines to match them.

goose mouse child man die foot

men geese dice children feet mice

But, some words stay the same:

one sheep  two sheep 

Words that rhyme

To recognise words that rhyme.

Words that rhyme are words that sound the same. They often have the same letter endings, like **big** and **dig**, **cat** and **hat**.

Draw lines to join two words that rhyme with the picture clue words.

fan

shell

hen

sun

tell pan men can

ten run fun fell

To recognise and spell words that rhyme.

Words that rhyme

Look at the pictures and spell the words. Draw lines to join words that rhyme.

sheep ____ ______ ___ ____

make sleep log

lock light bake

keep frog clock night

Make lists of rhyming words. It's fun and it will help your child to recognise spelling patterns.

Number words

To spell number words one to twenty.

Spell the numbers one to ten.
Spell each number word twice.

one	_ _ _	_ _ _
two	_ _ _	_ _ _
thr _ _	_ _ _ _ _	_ _ _ _ _
f _ _ r	_ _ _ _	_ _ _ _
f _ v _	_ _ _ _	_ _ _ _
six	_ _ _	_ _ _
s _ v _ n	_ _ _ _ _	_ _ _ _ _
ei _ _ _	_ _ _ _ _	_ _ _ _ _
n _ n _	_ _ _ _	_ _ _ _
t _ n	_ _ _	_ _ _

Now spell the numbers eleven to twenty.
Spell each number word twice.

el _ v _ n	_ _ _ _ _ _	_ _ _ _ _ _
tw _ lve	_ _ _ _ _ _	_ _ _ _ _ _
thirt _ _ n	_ _ _ _ _ _ _ _	_ _ _ _ _ _ _ _
fourt _ _ n	_ _ _ _ _ _ _ _	_ _ _ _ _ _ _ _
fif _ _ _ _	_ _ _ _ _ _ _	_ _ _ _ _ _ _
six _ _ _ _	_ _ _ _ _ _ _	_ _ _ _ _ _ _
seven _ _ _ _	_ _ _ _ _ _ _ _ _	_ _ _ _ _ _ _ _ _
eight _ _ n	_ _ _ _ _ _ _ _	_ _ _ _ _ _ _ _
n _ n _ teen	_ _ _ _ _ _ _ _	_ _ _ _ _ _ _ _
tw _ nty	_ _ _ _ _ _	_ _ _ _ _ _

To spell days of the week.

Days of the week

Day is an **ay** word. So is **today**.
Write **day** to spell the days of the week.
Spell each word twice.

Sun _ _ _ _ _ _ _ _ _ _

Mon _ _ _ _ _ _ _ _ _ _

Tues _ _ _ _ _ _ _ _ _ _ _ _

Wednes _ _ _ _ _ _ _ _ _ _ _ _ _ _ _

Thurs _ _ _ _ _ _ _ _ _ _ _ _ _

Fri _ _ _ _ _ _ _ _ _ _

Satur _ _ _ _ _ _ _ _ _ _ _ _ _

What day is it today? Today is ______________________.

My favourite day is ______________________.

Learn to spell these important words by heart.

Months of the year

To spell the months of the year.

Learn to spell the months of the year.
Spell each month twice.

Jan _ _ _ _

_ _ _ _ _ _ _ _ _

Febr _ _ _ _

_ _ _ _ _ _ _ _ _ _

Mar _ _

_ _ _ _ _ _

Apr _ _

_ _ _ _ _ _

M _ _

_ _ _

J _ n _

_ _ _ _ _

Jul _

_ _ _ _ _

Augu _ _

_ _ _ _ _ _ _ _

Sept _ _ _ _ _

_ _ _ _ _ _ _ _ _ _ _ _

Octo _ _ _

_ _ _ _ _ _ _ _ _

Nov _ _ _ _ _

_ _ _ _ _ _ _ _ _ _

Dec _ _ _ _ _

_ _ _ _ _ _ _ _ _ _

Spell the month we are in now. ____________________

Spell the month of your birthday. ____________________

Look for spelling patterns, e.g. September, November and December have the same endings.